Siblg

by the same authors

Families of Adults with Autism
Stories and Advice for the Next Generation
Edited by Jane Johnson and Anne Van Rensselaer
Foreword by Stephen Edelson, Autism Research Institute, San Diego
ISBN 978 1 84310 885 6
eISBN 978 1 84642 766 4

of related interest

You Are Special Too
A Book for Brothers and Sisters of Children Diagnosed with
Asperger Syndrome
Josie Santomauro
Illustrated by Carla Marino
ISBN 978 1 84130 656 2
eISBN 978 1 84642 929 3

Special Brothers and Sisters
Stories and Tips for Siblings of Children with Special Needs,
Disability or Serious Illness
Edited by Annette Hames and Monica McCaffrey
ISBN 978 1 84310 383 7
eISBN 978 1 84642 145 7

Voices from the Spectrum
Parents, Grandparents, Siblings, People with Autism, and
Professionals Share Their Wisdom
Edited by Cindy N. Ariel and Robert A. Naseef
ISBN 978 1 84310 786 6
eISBN 978 1 84642 446 5

Siblings and Autism
Stories Spanning Generations and Cultures
Edited by Debra L. Cumberland and Bruce E. Mills
ISBN 978 1 84905 831 5
eISBN 978 0 85700 295 2

Brotherly Feelings
Me, My Emotions, and My Brother with Asperger's Syndrome
Sam Frender and Robin Schiffmiller
ISBN 978 1 84310 850 4
eISBN 978 1 84642 594 3

Siblings

THE AUTISM

SPECTRUM

THROUGH

OUR EYES

Jane Johnson and Anne Van Rensselaer

Jessica Kingsley *Publishers*
London and Philadelphia

First published in 2010
by Jessica Kingsley Publishers
73 Collier Street
London N1 9BE, UK
and
400 Market Street, Suite 400
Philadelphia, PA 19106, USA

www.jkp.com

Copyright © Jane Johnson and Anne Van Rensselaer 2010

Printed digitally since 2015

Library of Congress Cataloging in Publication Data
A CIP catalog record for this book is available
from the Library of Congress

British Library Cataloguing in Publication Data
A CIP catalogue record for this book is
available from the British Library

ISBN 978 1 84905 829 2
eISBN 978 0 85700 281 5

Contents

Part II:
For Teenagers and Parents

Preface

The brothers and sisters who wrote this book think it helps to know that there are people who understand—really understand—what it's like to have a sibling with autism, and so they wanted to talk about how they feel. There are sibling support groups, where people can share these feelings, but not everybody lives near one. So if you're a sibling, this book is for you. You won't feel exactly like everybody who wrote a chapter, but we think you'll feel like you've just met someone who knows exactly how you feel by the end of this book. You're not alone.

Jane Johnson and Anne Van Rensselaer

Part I

*For Younger Children
and Parents*

1

Christopher Castaldi-Moller and Joshua Vazquez, Age 10

Christopher and Joshua

We're Christopher and Joshua.

We met at St. Patrick's school in Bay Ridge when we were in nursery, just three years old.

We became best friends and have been best friends ever since. We're ten years old now. (Mom's note: Little did Chris and Josh know at that time they would have much more in common than just liking Spider-Man! Christopher already had his nine-month-old baby brother William then, and Joshua's baby brother Justin came along when Josh was in kindergarten.)

The thing about us that makes our friendship special is that we both have brothers with special needs. Both of our brothers are on the autism spectrum. Both brothers go to special schools and follow special diets. In fact, everything about them has the word "special" in it! (Mom's note: The "diet" is the gluten-free/casein-free diet advocated by the Autism Research Institute—gluten is the protein in wheat, rye, and barley, and casein is the protein in milk.)

We decided we would like to write this chapter because being able to talk to each other helped us, so maybe we can help you too…

Chris

Hi, it's me, Chris. My little brother William is seven years old and he has ASD. ASD means he has an autism spectrum disorder. William is doing very well for a kid with autism. He can talk (even though he talks loud and sometimes he doesn't really make sense), he can read, and he can write. He goes to a school called School for Language and Communication Development (SLCD). But get this—he has to go on a bus for an hour each way to get there. One thing I know about schools for kids like William is that there aren't many around. The good thing is he loves being on a bus. The other good thing is that he goes to a school that's good for him; he learns there. He wouldn't do so well in a school like St. Patrick's, because it goes at a faster pace than he can learn at.

He's a good brother, but he hits me and pinches me. Sometimes when he does, I get really frustrated. Especially when he's not in such a good mood and starts complaining about—well, just about everything. It's hard to always understand that he can't control himself. In fact, I think he hurts me on purpose! But that's only part of the time. He's still a good brother. When he's in a good mood, we do have fun together. We watch movies together and he loves to swim with me.

I've noticed that he's in a bad mood when he eats things he's not supposed to eat, like bread. This is why he's on a special diet. But that means that whenever we go out to eat we have to make sure there's something there for him to eat, or else we have to take his special food with us. Usually the restaurants are OK with us bringing his food. We do this because we can't be sure the restaurants have the kind of food that's OK for him to eat.

Going out at all is an improvement from the old days, when we couldn't go out to eat ever because William couldn't take being in new places. Just bringing him into a crowded room would seem to make his skin crawl. Because he couldn't talk, he'd scream, cover his ears, and throw himself to the ground. He'd run out the door at every chance. Things are better now. He doesn't do that any more. We can even go to eat at the hibachi restaurant (a restaurant where they grill food in the middle of the table), though he still gets a little scared of the fire. After he eats he paces, so there has to be a quick end to our dinner usually!

I think autism affects a person's personality, but unlike being psychotic it's more of a medical condition that can get better with time and the right foods.

There are some good things to say about autism—one thing is that when you're autistic you can be very artistic. For example, my brother writes a book series at school about a cat named Fluffy that he made up. He can do nice drawings for a kid his age. He loves music. He's in the chorus at school. He can sing at his school plays, and he likes to sing songs in church.

Sometimes I feel as if I'll have to take care of him when I grow up. I've asked my mother about that and she hopes that William will be able to take care of himself one day. But he still can't do things like cross the street, or get dressed alone, and I worry that he doesn't know when there's something dangerous around him. Still, then I realize that he can get better. He's so much better now than in the old days. He doesn't get sick so much any more. Though now he gets seizures and we have to worry about that too. But really, he's getting much better all the time. Maybe it's because he's getting older.

Josh

Hi, it's me, Josh. My brother Justin is five years old and he's on the spectrum. He's going to be going to the same school as Christopher's brother. He went to a special school before called William O'Conner, and that school helped him improve his communication. I know that at SLCD my brother is going to improve even more. The message is really to have hope. Your siblings can get better too.

I think one of the worst things about my brother is that he embarrasses me in public. He does stuff my other friends think is weird. Whenever my friends say bad things about him, I just tell them my brother is a little different, and to just deal with it.

One of my friends has a little brother too. Justin is very good friends with that boy, even though he's not autistic. It makes me happy that he has friends who are not autistic, and that he can fit in with kids who are OK. It means he likes to have his own friends too.

Justin has to eat gluten-free foods, and he can't have things with milk in them. My mother is always reading labels and buying things she knows he can eat. Some of the stuff isn't bad! He likes to eat rice—that's gluten-free. He has to take a lot of vitamins. He's a picky eater. A lot of times, when I get food he can't have, like an ice cream cone, I feel bad. I know he wishes he could eat that food too, but if he ate it, his stomach would hurt. He'd get cranky, and it makes him get diarrhea.

When he's at home, he usually just watches TV or looks at the computer. But lately he tries to play with me. Sometimes he even tries to play rock-paper-scissors. He likes to play running races, and his favorite character is SpongeBob. Usually at night he'd like to watch TV with me, but then he doesn't want to go to sleep. It's important for him to get as much sleep as he can.

I hope one day he'll be completely better. I'm not sure about that, but if we all help him, he's going to improve for sure.

The thing that bugs us the most about our brothers is that we can't ever seem to play by ourselves without our brothers getting involved. The other thing is that they can hit us without warning and run away! It hurts! (And they never seem to get in trouble for it.) The thing that worries us the most about our brothers is that they might not ever get completely better. The thing that makes us happy about our brothers is that with hard work they *have* been getting better, especially behaviorally. Lately just by watching us, they can learn.

Here are some dos and don'ts. DON'T instigate, don't give them food they can't eat. Don't hit them back when they hit you, don't push them away from you if they ask you to do something. Don't get mad at your friends for not understanding, don't think that because your sibling is different that *you* are "weird" too. Don't be mad at them when they're not in the best of moods. Don't use them like they're your puppet, and don't expect them to do things the way other kids do—you can't change who they are. Don't yell at them. Don't give up.

DO tell them when you're upset, even if you think they don't understand you, because they *do* understand you. Do ask for your stuff back when they take it—they can't just take over the house. Do help them try again when they don't do well at something. Do be patient. Do try to include them in things that are fun—they love fun! Do try and stop them from getting overloaded—lower the TV sound, give them their favorite toy or possession, shut the blinds if it's too bright. Do talk to your parents when you think you need your parents too; the kid with autism can take up a lot of time and attention, but you'll need some time from your parents too. Do have some alone time to get away from them if it's, well, just getting too much to handle that day. Do try and include them with your friends if you can, because a lot of the time they don't have their own friends and being social is really important for them.

We're lucky that our brothers are getting better, because we know that not all kids get better. But we know what it's like in both cases, so let us know if you want to talk. You can email us at talkjoshandchris@aol.com.

2

Carley Belknap, Age 9

Bailey and Carley

It's not easy having a little brother. He wants all of your parents' attention, he never wants to watch the same movie as you do, and he borrows all of your toys without asking. It's more than a sister can handle sometimes! I have more to handle than the average big sister. My name is Carley and I'm nine years old. My brother Bailey is seven, and he has autism. That means that, in addition to all the regular brother stuff, he does a few extra annoying things: has trouble speaking, makes loud noises, plays with the same things over and over, rips paper, wakes up early—the list goes on and on…

It takes a lot of hard work and patience to be Bailey's sister. I have to repeat myself before my brother will listen, and sometimes I can't understand what he's saying to me. I have to go along to his doctor and therapy appointments, which means long car rides. I can't have some of my favorite foods in the house, because they're not on Bailey's special diet. Bailey likes to do the same things over and over, but that feels boring to me. At times, I have to keep my room locked, because Bailey will rip up my books. Other times, I have to sleep in the basement, because Bailey wakes up early and makes so much noise! Sometimes my ears hurt because of his loud crying, and I have to wear earplugs to block out the noise. Bailey makes loud noises when we're out in public, and that gets a little embarrassing. Sometimes I have to explain Bailey's behavior to people who don't understand autism. Once, he even took off all his clothes at the swimming pool, but that was pretty funny. Sometimes my world feels as if it revolves around Bailey, and it makes me feel mad at him!

Other times, my family tries to make special time just for me. Every Saturday my dad coaches my soccer team. My dad and I love to go to baseball games together, too. I love to do art projects with my mom, like painting or clay. Mom and I go running together, and we even compete in races sometimes. I love to tell jokes and put on puppet shows at home. We even built a secret clubhouse in our storage closet, and it says "No Boys Allowed." We have a special "Daughter Day" when I can go out to a restaurant for my favorite foods. When we go to the movies, sometimes I get to bring a friend along. Mom always helps me with my homework, and we read together each night after Bailey goes to bed. My brother and I go to different schools, so at school I can just be myself and not Bailey's sister. It's nice to have some time that belongs to me, and it's nice to take a break from autism.

Some days are tough, but Bailey is still my brother and I'll always love him. I guess all brothers and sisters have a hard time getting along sometimes. In a lot of ways, we're just regular kids, and hanging out with Bailey can be fun. He never lies to me, and sometimes he even does what I say. He loves it when I tickle him, and it makes him laugh so hard! We play tag and basketball together. We both like the trampoline, the swings, bike rides, swimming, climbing trees, going for walks, and vacationing at the beach. We both dislike shopping, so we gang up on Mom to make sure she never takes us along! We like to go to friends' houses for dinner. My friends all know Bailey has autism, and to them it's no big deal. I don't always get to spend time with my friends, but my friends are really good ones and they understand. Bailey is a really funny kid, and he makes me laugh. We have a lot in common, and I'm lucky to have him as my brother.

I've learned a lot from having a brother with autism. I know I'm not the only one. There are lots of kids like me, who have a brother or sister with autism, who have to deal with the same frustrations as I do. Some kids probably have a harder situation than me, and that makes me remember to be thankful for the things my brother can do. I've learned to be kind, patient, caring, and creative. I can do some sign language and I can understand Bailey's speech better than most people. I treat people with special needs just like anybody else. I appreciate things that other kids might not, like peace and quiet, or the chance to laugh and talk with my friends. I think about other people's feelings more. I work hard and try my best, even if it's not perfect. I know how to talk about my feelings. I think it's a big deal when my brother talks to me, and I'm a good listener. Most of all, I know I'm a really good sister and how much my family loves me.

When I grow up, I might like to be an artist, or an architect, or a writer. I might like to travel around the world. I might even help other families with kids who've been affected by autism, like mine. It will be my choice. Sometimes I think it isn't fair that I have to live with autism at my house, but I know I can help to change the future. My wish is for no more kids to have autism in the future. My brother didn't have a choice when it comes to living with autism. I guess that makes me the lucky one.

Carley, Dad, and Bailey

3

Cassidy Parker Knight, Age 13

Griffin and Cassidy

I'm Cassidy and I'm 13. I have an older brother—he's almost 15—and he has autism. He can't talk very clearly and he's in the special education program. It's always seemed strange to me that he's older than I am when he's so childlike. He watches the Disney classics, even the princess ones, and I think, "I'm too old for those. Why isn't he?" He watches *Teletubbies* and *Sesame Street* with my baby brother, and I think, "Why does he like those shows? They're for babies!"

The truth is, I don't really know the scientific reason why he likes those things. There are probably theories out there about why people with autism tend to like cartoons. But, mostly, I just know he likes the singing and dancing—so much, in fact, that he watches them over and over and over for long periods of time. And when I say that, I'm not saying he watches the same ten-second clip several times a day for a couple of days. I'm saying he watches the same ten-second clip *all the time* for many months, to the point where we have to buy him headphones for his computer to get the constant sound of "Ladybugs' Picnic" out of our heads.

I remember the first time—or one of the first times—I had a friend over at my house. I was in first grade, and her name was Vivian. It was the first time she had come over, and we were playing with dolls or whatever—I don't really remember—and my brother came running out completely naked. Now, Griffin hated wearing clothes. At that point, it was a chore to get him to wear clothes to school, let alone at home, so I'd seen him naked before. And I was only in first grade, so I didn't realize Vivian wouldn't have been exposed to that. She screamed, "Euwww! He's naked!" and my parents came running out and took care of it. It hurts my head to think of what Vivian told her mother when she got home that night. To this day, I don't know what she said, or what her mom thought about the whole thing, and I really don't want to.

Another time, I taught him a dance. I was in fourth grade, and I did ballet. Students at the Ballet Austin Academy were allowed to have small roles in their annual production of *The Nutcracker*. That year, I was to be a mouse. I went to rehearsal every Saturday for several months to learn and perfect the dance. It was a huge deal to be in this, because the show was put on by the professional dancers in the company. And I taught him my dance. I spent hours trying to teach Griffin how to do this dance, and he finally got it. He added his own sound effects to the dance; I still have no idea where he got them. He'd say, "Boo," and then he'd count to four (except it was hard to understand), then he'd say, "Together, apart." Except it sounded like "Geh-geh, apah." And he still remembers the dance, four years later. He hasn't done it recently, but I know he'd remember. All I would have to say is "Griffin, let's do the mouse dance." And he'd start. "Boo. Wa. Too. Fee. Fow. Geh-geh, apah." And he'd be doing the movements, too. Sometimes he'd get frustrated with me over it. But I stuck with it and made him perform it for all the relatives when they came over for Christmas.

I could go on and on about things Griffin has done, things I've done with him or taught him to do. I have a whole list of fond memories of him, and I have an even longer list of rip-your-hair-out memories of him. Sometimes I wonder what he'd be like if he were just like all my friends' older brothers. That's when I realize that he *is*. I love him, but he's always doing something that bugs me. I get mad at him and wish he were someone else's brother and not mine, and then I feel really bad but I know I don't mean it, and then I start thinking, "This is how it is for girls my age with brothers his age who don't have autism, right?"

My friend has an older brother, a little older than Griffin, but not much older. She's constantly complaining about something he did, and sometimes she tells me she wishes he'd just go away. But she has fun with him, too. So what I think is this: having a brother with autism is different—I can't truthfully say it's not—but it's never as bad as you think it is. You wish you could wring his neck for something annoying he did, then you wish someone would wring your neck for even thinking that. But other people feel that way too. Sure, other people don't have to hide their make-up from their brothers so they don't eat it, but I can assure you that people with normal brothers—or sisters, even—feel as if no one has it as bad as they do as far as siblings go, and theirs is the absolute worst there is. So we're in the same boat as them, just a little more extreme.

4

Maya Cassandra King, Age 10

Maya

Introduction

Hi, my name's Maya Cassandra King. Call me Maya. I'm about ten and a half years old, and I love animals and plants. When I grow up, I want to care for them.

That's not the reason I'm in this book. I'm not the reason at all. You're reading this because my brother, Jordan

McKechnie King, has autism. I'm here to tell you not about just him, but about the way he affects our whole family.

I don't want you to think of me as a "poor little girl with an autistic brother." Think of me as your friend. See the good side of me. See me as who I am, and not who my brother is. Don't look at me from the side through the corner of your eye. Confront me—I won't bite you. This is my story. A gift, to you.

Meet my family

Let me introduce you to my family. We're not what you would call peas in a pod. No, more like apples on a tree. We're all very close, but we're also on different branches. My dad builds musical instruments called marimbas—he makes them in our basement. Dad knows a lot about math and technology. His name is Fred.

Mom has a cool job—she's an African marimba teacher! She instructs many bands. She's also a great teacher to Jordan and me. Her name is MyLinda.

Jordan is older than I am by about 15 months. He has many athletic hobbies such as shaking our play structure by swinging, climbing, and playing on our homemade trapeze.

We all have our differences, and they can bring us closer together.

We stick together, like these trees

Problems that autism causes

Autism causes many things to happen that wouldn't happen otherwise. For instance, with autism, people need more help doing everyday things. This can make you feel jealous, angry, or abandoned. When Jordan is acting up, my parents have to take care of him even when I have something important to share.

Sometimes I felt put aside when Jordan got to go to fun places for kids with autism. He used to go to a special place I called "the place with the giant playgrounds and a waiting room." The grown-ups called it Occupational Therapy at Neurotherapeutics. I'm not sure what that means, and I don't care. The whole place was so unfair to me—thinking about it makes me boil bright red inside. Jordan got to play in plastic ball pits, and go on big swings, and do all these incredible playground things with a woman specializing in autism. Where was I during this? I was sitting on an old couch, reading boring books or playing stupid waiting-room games. Sometimes I would say I had to use the restroom, and that gave me a good excuse to go on the enormous playground. Then I would pick up a toy left on the floor, or sit on a swing, or climb a bit. I don't feel very guilty for doing this, because it was so unfair.

If I asked permission to swing, I was still called back to the hated old couch. Once I asked the woman who worked with Jordan if I could play; after Jordan was done, I began flying on the swing—not just sitting, or swinging, but *flying!* But my glory was short-lived, because we had to go home.

Sometimes I've been blamed for things Jordan did. This doesn't happen much any more. Jordan would break something or make a ton of noise, and I would be told that I shouldn't annoy Jordan and cause him to get in trouble, or make him do something he shouldn't. Once he even flushed my prescription glasses down the toilet! Until Dad unbolted the toilet from the floor, I was blamed for *two weeks* for losing them.

It feels great to confide in you and say all these things. It's unfair. Resentment. Anger. Autism.

Jordan's strange habits

Lots of kids have habits like nail-biting, not speaking right, or collecting things like rocks or cards, but Jordan isn't like that. He does things you normally wouldn't see kids his age, or any age, doing. I don't have space to list all the strange things he does. Besides clogging up the toilet with just about *anything,* Jordan causes lots of weird problems that he wouldn't without autism. Jordan always gets a talking-to after he does something bad, but that doesn't keep him from doing it again.

He usually has two fat Disney storybooks in the crook of his arm—the kind with big pictures, multiple stories, and lots of pages. He flips the pages over and over, sometimes pausing to look at a picture. The repetitive flipping noise doesn't bother us. I sort of like it. What bothers us is people staring at us in public places like restaurants and movie theaters.

Maya and Jordan

I think Jordan hums and keeps his hands by his face for comfort. Right now, Dad is teaching him to keep his hands down, and Mom is working on his table manners.

My classmates sometimes act weird around Jordan, but I can always count on my best friends to be helpful and understanding. What really gets me is when people make faces at him, or when they ask questions about him in a mean voice. But from my ten years with Jordan, I've learned some big life lessons, like patience, and, surprisingly, quietness.

Releases from stress

I think it's important to release all of your emotional stress. No matter if you're the sibling, the parent, or the relative, or if you're the disabled person, the anger and sadness should be released. If it isn't, family problems can start. Take it from me.

Sports, racing, or just walking through the park are a big help. They not only cure the need to be outside more, but can also increase health and can help make strong friendships with your teammates. Building up pride and self-esteem helps heal any situation. Knowing you're part of a team is a feeling unmatched by anything.

Learning a new skill such as art, science, music, or nature awareness takes your mind off family troubles—it's good to focus on new subjects. This frees your mind of worries and doubts, replacing them with wonders, curiosity, and hopes.

After a particularly bad incident, try relaxing in a comfortable, familiar place by yourself. Once you feel ready to confront somebody, remember to be chilled, and think of what you're going to say.

Finding a new furry, slimy, or scaly best friend can be one of the best ways to take your mind off autism! A pet will not only help you but the Jordan in your family as well. Jordan has learned to be gentle with our cats, and to be responsible by feeding our fish.

Making a strong bond with anyone or anything—whether it's cats, soccer, baseball, football, fish, sculpting, painting, singing, or anything else—can help mend a hurting heart.

Spending time with animals helps...everyone (Jordan and Maya)

Big life lessons

I've learned many life lessons from ten years on the planet with Jordan, and I would like to share them with you.

Trust is a very important key. Knowing who and what to trust, where and when, has taught me a lot, as it will you.

Having a bright, cheery sense of humor helps soften and light up any dark situation. Don't overuse it, though!

Friendship really is a ship. It can sail far and wide, if it's navigated and steered right. My friends always support me. I've even become a friend to Jordan!

If you sport a good attitude along with the traits above, there isn't a situation that can stop you! (I know this is the advice usually given by grown-ups, but remember: this is coming from me, a growing ten-year-old girl!)

Adios, goodbye, and see you later

Now that I've shared my story with you, I might as well mosey on home. Please don't forget my family, my story, or me. I hope sharing these personal annoying, frustrating, and embarrassing events of my everyday life will help you realize you aren't alone.

I've told you about my life coping with autism and its challenges. I'm looking forward to a cure for autism. I want to hear what Jordan and all those other kids have to say.

5

Chandra Kelley-Robinson, Age 11

Chandra and Christopher

My name's Chandra and I'm 11. I have a four-year-old brother named Christopher who most likely has autism. From my understanding, autism is a brain development problem that usually delays communication and motor skills. Despite these challenging characteristics, my brother is very lovable! I have a great time with him.

Our day consists of many things. Last weekend, for example, Christopher awoke at about 3 a.m. This caused the entire family to wake up earlier than normal—including me. The first thing Christopher did when he saw me was sit on my feet and hug my knees. We think he does this to soothe his stomach or because he's imitating a TV show. Later that same day, Christopher ate many of his favorite gluten-free/casein-free foods—many of which are not my favorites, but we try to support his diet as much as we can.

My little brother doesn't talk in complete sentences. Instead, he "scripts." That means he repeats stuff he's already heard. For example, he sometimes repeats phrases from television programs, like *Elmo's World, Go Diego Go,* and *Dora the Explorer*. It makes sense because he usually says the stuff in context.

All in all, Christopher is the best little brother and I wouldn't ask for him to be changed at all!

6

Alyssa Chmura, Age 19

Alyssa

I've been my brother's sister for 16 years, for all but three years of my life. Being a sister is part of my character, part of me, just as much as my love of music, sense of humor, constant reading habit, and passion for teaching, my intended career. Although my brother has been diagnosed as "autistic" for about ten years, I don't like to think in those terms. The word autistic is an adjective, a descriptor of the nature or character of a noun. I never use the word "autistic" to describe my brother for precisely that reason: autism is *not* a part of him; it's merely something he has to deal with. Autism isn't part of his identity in the way being his sister is part of mine. Some people can't see past the diagnosis to understand the person underneath. My brother is still a loving, goofy, intelligent, stubborn teenager despite having autism, and I love him all the more for it. I sometimes imagine what our lives would be like had we not received the news of his condition a decade ago. Interestingly enough, my projected image of the life our family could have had is quite similar to the one we do have—full of love, laughs, occasional arguments, but essentially close-knit. I always come to the conclusion that I love our life the way it is—although autism presents us with many challenges, typical life would too, and we meet these challenges together as a family.

Another part of my character is my need for organization and my love of lists, so I've decided to include, along with my reflections on siblinghood, a list of things to remember when dealing with a sibling with autism. This list is made up of things I've learned over the years, things I wish I'd been told from the start, but probably wouldn't have taken to heart so much had I not learned through firsthand experience. I hope those who read this book will find my list helpful and will be able to relate to and gain confidence from the points I bring up.

Important facts about living with a sibling with autism

1. Life probably wouldn't be half as interesting or full of laughter if your sibling were "normal."

2. If you play off your sibling's atypical behavior as no big deal when he or she acts up in public, other people will follow your lead. Acting embarrassed or getting angry will only draw more attention to the situation.

3. It will surprise you how typical your relationship will be with your sibling. You'll probably argue over the remote control, computer, who broke what, etc., just as much as typical kids. Sibling squabbles transcend autism.

4. Be proud of your sibling, no matter how annoying, embarrassing, and infuriating he or she can be. Even though he or she might not be able to express it, he or she is proud to be your sibling too.

5. You shouldn't really have to explain your sibling to your friends. If they're truly good friends, they'll make the effort to understand your sibling and will treat him or her as well as (or maybe better than!) you do.

6. It's important to have inside jokes with your sibling. It will make both of you feel special to have something that's just between the two of you. Plus, humor transcends autism, too.

7. Of course, you need to spend quality time with your sibling, but, just like typical kids, he or she needs space. Alone time for both of you is important.

8. Although sometimes your sibling's condition is too much for you to handle and you find yourself asking, "Why can't he/she just be NORMAL?" think about how your sibling feels. You only have a front-row seat to the condition he or she lives with every day. He or she

lives in a state of dependence, not able to think about and react to the world the way we do. Deep down, subconsciously perhaps, he or she yearns for so-called "normalcy" too, probably more than you do.

9. Most of all, remember that your most important job in life is not whatever career you pursue, but to be the best sibling you can be. Be supportive, helpful, strong, silly, patient, even-tempered, proud, compassionate, enthusiastic, and always full of love. Your sibling will be eternally grateful and reciprocate your efforts to the best of his or her ability.

7

Cami Poole, Age 10¹¹⁄₁₂

Cami

My name is Cami and I'm almost 11 years old. I have two brothers, Aidan and Davis. Davis is five years old and Aidan is six years old.

Aidan is somewhere in the range of autism, but we're not certain if he's autistic or not. He has other problems too, such as speech and sensory issues.

Aidan's problems keep me from doing things I want to do. For example, my family can't go to the pool and stay for as long as we want. Aidan will throw a fit after we've been there for only 45 minutes. He'll kick a random person or push down a little kid. I get *so* frustrated when Aidan is like that. I also can't have a friend at my house without Aidan pushing, kicking, hugging, and licking them. A lot of times Aidan will scream very loud when we're at home. When he does that everyone only pays attention to *him* and not *me*. I get so mad at Aidan because on evenings like that, after Aidan is calm, he gets *hugs and kisses* and Davis and I are sent to bed! I can't believe Aidan gets everything! At times like that, I feel invisible. Sometimes I wish I lived somewhere else far away from Aidan. But after I'm mad at him, he's really sweet and I like him again. It's weird how it's like that, but I suppose I'm used to the situation now. But that doesn't mean I like it that way. I still get really annoyed with him and wish someone would understand how frustrating it is. Aidan is still my brother, though, and I love him, as I do Davis. I guess it's not *all* bad—Davis could have problems too! Then both of my brothers would be like that. No thanks! I think this current situation is better than that one.

If other kids out in public see Aidan acting the way he does, I get looked at as if I'm like him. I'm *not* like him. I'm a separate person. I get really embarrassed. At the same time, I get upset too, because these kids are mean to Aidan. He doesn't see that they're not accepting of him. I wish those kids would be more open-minded to other kids who have differences. Maybe they just don't understand how to be tolerant of others who aren't like them.

Even though I've experienced some difficult times in my life because Aidan is my brother, I feel I'm mature for my age and will be able to understand more about life issues in the future because of him.

Davis, Cami, and Aidan

8

Ben Jepson, Age 13

Ben and Aaron

My name is Ben Jepson. I'm 13 years old and my father is Dr. Bryan Jepson, who works at Thoughtful House Center for Children and treats patients with autism. I was first introduced to autism when my younger brother Aaron was diagnosed with it in 2001. He used to follow me around all of the time and did whatever I did. After he regressed, he rarely looked at me. But after years of treatment, he's gotten so much better. He can now communicate with us and participate in family activities.

I never really paid attention to how different Aaron was when I was little—I thought it was just his personality. But when I got a bit older, some of my friends thought he was stupid (which is definitely not true), and liked to make fun of him sometimes. I told them that he's autistic and taught them a little about autism. They understood and apologized immediately.

It was always embarrassing when we took Aaron into a store, a movie theater, or just any public place when he was in a bad mood. He'd have meltdowns and would sometimes hit my parents or myself when he was furious. It usually wasn't his fault about his bad moods, because most of the time he was in excruciating pain from problems in his GI (gastrointestinal) tract, and I don't blame him. But still, it's never fun to be standing right next to a screaming kid with everybody staring at you.

In 2008, we saw a news story about a seven-year-old boy in foster care named Austin who had autism. Nobody else seemed to want him, but we saw we could help, so my family decided to adopt him. We thought he was going to be a pretty easy kid to take care of—boy, were we wrong. Austin was a screamer, and by screams, I mean unordinary screams. They were so loud that sometimes they didn't even sound human. I'd never been through anything so stressful in my life. It was definitely a test of patience. I wanted to leave the house a lot for the first couple of months that we had him, because I was sick of hearing him scream. Austin couldn't speak, so screaming was the way he communicated when he wanted something or didn't get his way. My parents didn't give in to it, so it just got worse and worse. I had moments where I thought we had no clue what we were doing, but I also knew inside that we were doing the right thing. Now that we've had him for a long time, he's recovered a lot with treatment. I can't imagine what life would be like without him now. He's usually a very happy kid, but he still has a lot of challenges, just like Aaron.

People with autism can have amazing minds and talents. I always think of Jason McElwain, the autistic high school basketball player who scored six three-pointers in four minutes when his coach let him play in the last game of the season. They just need to be given a chance.

Growing up with autism in my life has made me a better person in so many ways. I've learned to be kinder, to have patience, and to think differently about autism than most people. I love my brothers, and my parents for everything they've done and all of the sacrifices they've made, and I'm grateful for that.

9

Chelsea Lang, Age 17

Michael and Chelsea

Advice I wish I'd gotten

1. Ease up! Don't be so hard on yourself. You didn't do this, and it's nobody's fault your brother or sister thinks and acts differently!

2. Believe me, your parents don't expect you to be the "good" kid. Don't think you have to be better than you are right now, because you're exactly who you're

supposed to be. They'll love you even if you mess up really bad. One time in first grade, I flunked a spelling test. The words were so easy that I got really mad at myself for not studying. I remember thinking, "I'm smarter than this. It's OK for Michael to get bad grades, but I'm supposed to get As!" I got myself so worked up thinking how stupid I was that I didn't stop to count my blessings. Now that I'm older, I'm thankful my mind works like I need it to. And I still feel stupid sometimes! But I don't worry about what I'm "supposed" to know, or how I'm "supposed" to behave. I know that no matter what my brother might not know or how he might act sometimes, that doesn't affect how I do.

3. Laugh: at others, at yourself—it doesn't matter. If something's funny, you can laugh! People won't think you're a bad person if you laugh at something your brother or sister does, as long as you don't make fun of him or her on purpose to hurt his or her feelings.

4. Don't be embarrassed to be around your brother or sister. One day in fourth grade, we were at dinner in a restaurant—I think it was Ruby Tuesday's. Michael was flicking his lizard tail, something he always did at home. (He'd get toy lizards from the toy store and get Mom to cut the tail off so he could flick it, because he liked to see it wave in front of his face.) I remember that day it seemed as if everybody in the restaurant was staring at us. I could feel my face turning red, and I thought I would have a heart attack if people didn't stop looking. But then this baby started crying really loudly. I looked over, and the baby's mom looked just as embarrassed as I felt! Now I know that everybody gets embarrassed now and then, and you have to shrug it off. Even if people do laugh, it can't hurt you *unless you let it*. But if nobody makes a big deal out of it, like

Michael's flicking, then people will usually lose interest in it and not even pay attention.

5. Play with your brother or sister! Even if your brother or sister likes to do weird stuff for fun, or stuff that's just downright boring, you can find something you both like to do. Sometimes this is as easy as walking outside, but sometimes you have to get creative. When I was in second grade, Michael went through a phase where he'd play the *George of the Jungle* theme song over and over again. Whenever I tried to make him go outside to play on the swings with me, he'd yell and scream until he could go back inside. I got fed up with it really fast. Then one day Michael was in a really good mood, so I decided to take him outside on the swings again. I had him on the swing, and, of course, he started the whole yelling and screaming thing again. But I had a plan, and I could sing louder than he could yell. "George, George, George of the Jungle, strong as he can be! Watch out for that tree!" To me, it sounded really stupid. But Michael had stopped yelling and screaming and just sat there, waiting. So I kept going. "George, George, George of the Jungle, lives a life that's free!" Then, to my surprise, Michael yelled, "Watch out for that AHHHHHH... tree!" He sounded exactly like a copy of the soundtrack song. I was thrilled. For the next few days, all he wanted to do was "go outside and play on the George swing." (And yes, I did finally tell my parents what the "George swing" meant.)

6. Sometimes you have to look out for him or her. Now, it's not your job to be your sibling's bodyguard 24/7, but remember, not everybody will be kind to your brother or sister. Even if your brother or sister is older than you, they might need some special looking-out-for in certain cases. If you see some kids bullying your brother

or sister, *go tell an adult*. Don't put yourself in danger. If somebody is physically beating up your special-needs brother or sister, you can find someone to help. In the movies, the kid getting bullied is left by himself, and nobody helps him until his brother or sister comes in later, after he's hurt, and gives him a pep talk. Then he learns to stand up for himself, and next time the bullies come back, he stands up to them and they all run off crying. *Life isn't a movie*. If somebody is bullying your brother or sister (and this doesn't just mean punching or kicking him; it can also mean stealing his special toy that he takes with him everywhere, or messing up his hair on purpose if the bully knows it really bothers him), or if somebody is hurting your brother or sister just to be mean, go find an adult to tell. Who cares if you're "snitching" or if they won't like you any more? That's *your family*, and you have to take care of your brother or sister.

7. Sometimes people will pick on you because of your brother or sister. I wish I could say nobody will ever tease you and everyone will accept your brother or sister (like good people should accept one another), but that's not the truth. When this happens, don't feel like you have to fight them. You're not a coward if you don't answer back. Trust me, they've just proved that they're the worst kinds of cowards in this world— cowards who pick on people just for being different. Yes, your brother or sister might be labeled as "mentally disabled," but that is *not* the same as "stupid." And don't fall for the whole "I just told the truth; he *is* stupid!" thing. Nobody else will believe these people; even their friends are not encouraging this kind of talk. When I was in sixth grade, this kid named Burton started picking on me because I'd written a story about my

brother for our English class assignment. He called me "special…as in 'Special Ed!'" and said my whole family was "retarded." It got to the point where I didn't want to go to school in the morning, because I'd have to sit next to him in the afternoon. One day, we had a big test, and I'd stayed up late studying. By that afternoon, I was too tired to be scared of Burton and his stupid comments. I don't remember what he said that day, but I do clearly remember slapping him in the face. I wasn't in huge trouble for it, but afterwards I felt so ashamed for stooping to his level when I could have just told my mom or my teacher about all the times he bullied me. The whole point of this story is to tell you that you don't have to lower yourself by fighting their way. Again, it isn't snitching if it's *your family*. You're better than they are, so you deserve not to have to put up with their dumb insults. Tell your teacher, or your parents, or your counselor—anyone who will put a stop to it.

10

Micah Quindazzi, Age 14

Micah

Autistic kids—some people think they're weird, but I believe they're just different. My brother, Philip, is diagnosed with PDD-NOS, which falls in the middle of the autism

50

spectrum. I'm here to share my experiences, insights, and some advice on how to deal with your siblings.

Living with a 17-year-old brother with autism has given me a lifetime of experience. Ever since I was little, I noticed my brother wouldn't respond to "Don't." To him, it meant "Do it." Often that would lead to exactly the opposite of what I intended. I have no idea why my brother does this, but I've learned to use different words. Giving Philip choices helps him respond positively and understand the right direction to go. He needs consistency, since he doesn't deal with change well. He has anxiety and will get stuck, digging his heels in. I give Philip space to continue his daily routine; if I need to ask him to change, I introduce the idea but I understand it's his choice whether or not to respond. Whatever you do, don't move a toy or change the TV channel—just keep it consistent.

Going out to a restaurant, theme park, or even the grocery store can end abruptly if Philip freaks out. We can plan the day, cover all the bases, explain the day to him, but we just never know when he'll explode. This can be frustrating if I'm having a great time, but fantastic when I just want to go home myself. If your sibling is freaking out, don't egg them on as you're only going to escalate the situation. The best thing to do is leave them alone and give them space to calm down, and then your parents won't be upset with you.

Trying to play with your sibling can be a challenge. I've learned not to play anything aggressive or fool around, because he doesn't know when to stop, and things get out of hand.

I've noticed a lot of autistic people have a deep passion or interest in something. Have you noticed how they remember things or pick up things you don't see in a movie? If you stop and listen to them, they can prove to be insightful—they see things we often miss. They really are focused on the smallest details. Some of these insights have helped me deal with living with my autistic brother.

Philip

Accepting their autism helps you move on and you can start to see the person they are. Remember that staying negative breeds more negativity, and you'll make your own life more difficult. A key to dealing with most problems that come up is first to ask what they feel or think about the situation. Next, you verbally acknowledge their opinion. I've found it best not to share my opinion, because he stops listening. Then I re-evaluate both opinions. I find neutral ground or lean more to his side for the sake of peace. Is it best to be right or to make it work? If the situation does escalate, it's a good idea to walk away.

You *can* build a healthy relationship with your sibling! Find a common interest and talk about it. My brother loves *Star Wars*, and so I watch the movies with him for the twentieth time, or talk about them with him. It helps if you want to play board games or video games—it goes a lot smoother if it's based on an area he's fixated on. Spending some time and exercising patience helps to nourish a bond and makes your own life better.

I've shared some of my experiences, insights, and suggestions for how to deal with a sibling, and I hope these will help you as much as they've helped me in my life. In fact, having an autistic brother has helped me develop patience, tolerance of others, and the ability to use reason, which will greatly help me in my own life. The most important thing to remember is not to focus on the negative of living with a sibling with autism, but to strive to see the positives—try to see them as a person, and not as your problem.

11

Anonymous, Age 34

Growing up with a brother with an autism spectrum disorder wasn't always easy. There were frustrating times, when he just didn't *get* it, no matter how much I tried to explain something to him. There were times when he embarrassed me in front of my friends and classmates. There were times when I felt my parents were treating me unfairly, and they expected a lot more of me than of him. But of all of these things, nothing upset me more than the way other kids would tease my brother.

Because of his autism spectrum disorder, my brother sometimes said or did things that seemed weird to the other kids, and they would make fun of him because of it. Kids also figured out that my brother was very literal (and sometimes gullible), and they would get him into trouble by telling him to do things he shouldn't do. For example, one time, in the middle of class, they told him to jump out of the classroom window (luckily it was on the ground floor!). He did it, just because they told him to, and because he didn't know better. All the kids laughed because he had actually jumped out the window, and he got in trouble with the teacher. I used to get really mad that these things happened to my brother. He didn't deserve to be treated that way, and he certainly didn't deserve to be punished by his teachers, too! But I also felt guilty, because I never did anything to stop these things from happening. I'm not sure why I didn't—I think I was afraid that if I said something, the kids would make fun of me, too.

None of the kids at school knew my brother had a disability. They didn't understand that there was a reason he acted the way he did. If they'd known, maybe they would have been nicer to him. There were times when I wished I had the courage to tell them he couldn't help these things, and they shouldn't treat him that way.

As a kid, I think I focused a lot on the negatives—all the ways I wished my brother were different, or the things I wished I'd done differently in order to make life better for both of us. But now that I'm an adult, I see things a little bit differently. I see all the positive ways my brother has influenced my life. Because of him, I became a psychologist and decided to work with other kids with autism. Because of him, I decided to run support groups for siblings, to help other kids going through what I went through. And because of him, I'm a more patient, caring, and understanding person.

So if I can offer any advice, it's this: when you're feeling down about having a sibling with autism—when kids are being cruel, when your parents are being unfair, when your sibling is frustrating the heck out of you, when you're feeling guilty for not doing more, when you're feeling jealous for all the attention your sibling gets—remember there's a positive side, too. It's normal to feel all those negative things, but if you can find a positive way to deal with them (talking to your friends, your parents, participating in online discussion groups, or reading this book!), you'll one day realize how much stronger a person you are because of your experience as a sibling, and how much it's shaped your path in life. And maybe, like me, you'll decide you wouldn't want to trade it for anything.

12

Adam Barrett, Age 27

Heathar and Adam

My story starts when I was four years old, when my sister was rushed into the hospital. I didn't have a clue about what was happening, or the severity of my sister's illness. My mum and dad and our close family friends were all very supportive. But from that one afternoon 21 years ago, when a police car, ambulance, and fire engine (ordinarily a young boy's dream!) turned up at our house, my life would change forever. My sister contracted encephalitis—a rare brain inflammation caused by a virus, which resulted in an autistic-like disability. My little sister is unable to speak, has a profound hearing loss, a right-sided paralysis, and a seizure disorder.

Not for a single moment growing up did I feel neglected. This is due to the amazing parents who brought my sister and me into the world. They've dedicated their lives to finding the best for Heathar and me. Your family will find the strength and resolve to make your own family the very best. You might be the best at math or at gardening or even at bike-riding—who knows? You need to know it will bring out the very best in everyone in your family, and then having all of these wonderful people in your family—well, wow!

I knew my sister was not well and I wanted to help to get her better, like everyone else. I even promised my mother I would develop a "seizure gun" to stop Heathar's epilepsy. Growing up, Heathar and I formed a very close bond and enjoyed playing together in the house and getting up to mischief like most brothers and sisters do. Heathar couldn't copy me, but I quickly learned how to help her do things like jumping up and down on the bed. I just took her through the movements, and away we went.

From the very start of Heathar's life, I've been a very overprotective brother. If anyone looked at her in a disapproving manner, I would stare straight back at them and smile, as if to say, "What are you looking at?" This is a very difficult personality trait to subdue—it's a natural human reaction. I'm Heathar's big brother, therefore I have to protect her, whether she likes it or not. One of the major things I've learned while being with Heathar is that people take life too seriously. There have been numerous occasions when I've seen people take the utmost offense at the simplest of things. A light being switched off triggers panic and shock amongst the most helpful of shop assistants. Going through a door labeled "Staff only" seems like the end of the world for some people—there's no way back now! There are many examples I could list, but the point is you must first see the funny side of things, and not take any of the little autistic-like behaviors as serious.

Heathar has had a profound effect on my life, guiding my career and attitudes towards people who have a disability. I trained as a teacher, and also as a communication partner, and last as a tutor at a university, all owing to my beautiful sister's ability to inspire and motivate me. The same can happen with you, too.

One of the major things I've learned from Heathar is patience, and the second is tolerance. These are important, and I've needed them in abundance. We make sure we always stay positive and focus on all the good things in life, and let all the "negative nonsense" (Heathar's typed words) go.

Whatever it is your brother or sister with autism has done or is doing, put that into the bigger picture. Is it hurting anyone? Offending anyone? All can be rectified, and laughter will follow when you recount the day.

Forever I'll be in debt to my wonderful parents and my exceptional sister, who, despite being written off by many professionals at a very young age, continues to achieve, inspire, and amaze everyone who is lucky enough to know her. I wouldn't change you, dear sister, for the world! My sister has her own website—www.heatharashley.com—and you can follow her progress and also be inspired.

13

Missy Olive, Age 41

Melissa and Mac

I was 11 years old when my brother was born. I remember it as if it was just yesterday—I cried my eyes out. And at that point, I didn't even know he had autism. What I really wanted was a sister. I already had three brothers, and I certainly didn't need or want any more boys in the house. Of course, I would grow to love my brother even though he was not a girl. Surprisingly, he and I are closer than I am with any of my other brothers.

Over the years I've learned a lot of things, so I've developed a list of advice for you as you grow up with your sibling with autism.

Lesson 1: It's OK to be scared

My brother's story is probably different from most. He had some difficulty during delivery and he was unable to breathe for a few minutes. The lack of oxygen hurt his brain, which impacted his motor skills and caused him to have seizures. About 25 percent of children with autism have seizures. This can be a very scary thing.

There are many types of seizures. My brother has complex partial seizures. When he's having a seizure, it looks as if he isn't breathing because his lips turn blue and he makes a funny sound and moves his mouth funny. Other seizures, like grand mal seizures, can cause the person to fall down and shake on the floor. There's a type of seizure called absence seizures that make the person lose focus briefly.

The first few times he had a seizure at home, it scared my mother because we didn't know he was seizing—we just thought he wasn't breathing. Mac is now 30 and he still has seizures. They're still scary, but I know what to do now.

Your brother or sister might not have seizures but he or she might need to have IV (intravenous) medical treatment, or maybe screaming tantrums are frequent—these can also be scary. Having a sibling with autism will present you with many challenges, and it's OK to be scared when you face them.

Lesson 2: It's OK to treat your sibling with autism the way you treat your other siblings

One of the lessons I've learned over the years is to remember that Mac is my brother, and I should treat him the same way I treat my other brothers. Of course, he gets special attention due to his special needs, but he also gets gently teased. It's important to note that we didn't tease my brother because he had autism—we teased him because it was our right as siblings to treat him like we treated each other.

One of my favorite games to "play" with Mac was the animal sounds game. Mac had a "See'n Say" for farm animals. When you pulled the string, it said the animal's name and then produced the sound the animal made. For example, "The cat says meow." One day, by accident, I activated the cow. Mac had a funny look on his face, so I repeated what the toy said. Perhaps I accentuated the "moo" a bit louder than the toy, and perhaps I made it sound scary. Mac started crying. I thought this was funny, so I waited until he stopped crying and I did again. This became our little game. I would scare him, make him cry, and Mom would come running in to "save" him. He'd turn to look at me and I would do it again. Of course, I got in big trouble over that one. My mom yelled at me and told me to stop making him cry. She told me she never wanted to hear me make the cow sound again. Soon I learned that all I had to do was silently move my lips like I was saying the phrase, "The cow says mooooooooo," and Mac would cry. I couldn't get in trouble then. Our game continued over the years. Now he doesn't cry any more—he laughs. And he still asks me to make the cow sound. Whatever it is you do to your other siblings, it's OK to do to your sibling with autism.

Lesson 3: It's OK to stand up for your sibling

Thirty years ago when Mac was born, people weren't aware of autism, and they didn't understand why he made funny noises or moved in strange ways. I would like to think people today understand it because it's much more common, but unfortunately they don't. You'll meet people who will make fun of or bully your sibling. You might even meet someone who intentionally hurts him or her.

I've learned over the years that it helps to stand up for your sibling while also educating the offender. My brother and I have been out in stores, and children will be whispering, pointing, and laughing at Mac because he's rocking or acting strangely. I simply go over and say, "You seem to be really interested in my brother. Would you like to say hello to him?" This usually stops them in their tracks.

When you see someone treat your sibling inappropriately, you shouldn't get aggressive—hitting or hurting the offender won't help the situation and you could get in trouble. Yelling won't help either. The offender might think it's funny if he or she can get you mad. However, you can talk to the offender and try to teach him or her, and depending on the situation, you can get an adult to help you. Just remember, when someone does something mean to your sibling, it's most likely because he or she's scared or doesn't understand. The person will benefit from the help you or an adult provide.

Lesson 4: It's OK to use your sibling for things

Let's face it, growing up with a sibling with autism isn't easy. No one asked us if we wanted all those trips to the doctor, or if we wanted to eat special food (how many of your friends even know what gluten is?), or if we wanted to learn how to do applied behavior analysis (ABA)—

we should be able to get something out of the deal for ourselves.

Mac helps me in more ways than he knows. For example, he's great at taking out the trash. He's an expert at picking up things and putting them where they belong. He always shuts the doors and turns off the lights. However, the best help Mac has given me is in picking out my friends. Mac is the true test of friendship. I usually tell my friends about Mac long before I bring them over to the house. This gives them time to ask questions about my brother. I also tell funny stories about him so they won't be surprised if he does something odd. The bottom line is that good friends will understand why you want to sleep over at their house so you can get away, or why your sibling is still wearing diapers—they understand how hard it is to grow up with a sibling with autism.

Your sibling might offer all sorts of advantages for you. For example, access to special toys, extra dessert, or even a special sitter. He or she might be great at helping you with your homework or your music lessons—whatever special help or treat you get, it's OK.

Lesson 5: It's OK to get mad at your sibling

Our siblings with autism will do things that will cause us to get angry, and that's OK, too. As we grow up, we will get mad at all sorts of people, including our parents, siblings, friends, and teachers. The important thing to remember is that your sibling might not fully understand why you're mad.

My brother hates red lights. He also hates it when the car has stopped when it's supposed to be moving (for example, in traffic jams). When the car stops, he screams, rocks, and bites his hand. It makes me really mad because it's loud and it causes people to stare from the neighboring cars. Mac doesn't understand that his behavior upsets me. He thinks if he screams, the light will change and the car will go.

On the other hand, your sibling might know exactly why you're mad, and he or she might be doing the behavior on purpose. It's *really* OK to be mad then. The problem with this situation, though, is that if you get mad, it might cause your sibling to do the behavior more. For example, Mac loves to stand really close to me so he can try to put his finger in my face. He doesn't want anything when he does this—he's just doing it to make me mad. If I yell at him and tell him to stop, he does it again and again. He even laughs at me when I get mad.

Sometimes your sibling won't know he or she's making you mad, while other times he or she will be doing it on purpose. You need to know that it's OK to be mad and to get frustrated. Ask your parents to help you so you know how to deal with your frustration, and ask your parents to help you help your sibling to stop engaging in those behaviors.

Lesson 6: It's OK to get jealous of your sibling

Your sibling with autism is going to get extra help and extra attention because of his or her special needs. This might mean extra trips to the doctor, extra therapy appointments, special schools, or therapy in your home. All of this extra stuff is for your sibling and not for you, which might cause you to feel as if your sibling gets all of the attention.

When my brother was young, he had special therapy three days per week. Our family had to pile in the car and drive for 45 minutes just to get to the therapy. We stayed at therapy for almost four hours! While my brother and my mother were in therapy, my brothers and I had to stay in the childcare room with the other siblings. We didn't get special attention and we didn't get alone time with our mother, because she was always so busy with Mac. It made us feel very jealous.

Almost 30 years later, professionals have learned that siblings of children with autism need extra attention too. They're trained to help your parents make special time for you alone. There are now special programs for siblings and even special doctors who can help you talk through your feelings. Your sibling will most likely have a special plan at school called an Individual Education Plan (IEP). As part of this plan, your parents can request that someone from your school's staff talks to you about your feelings toward your sibling with autism.

Your brother or sister will have unique needs that will require different types of therapies. All of the attention that comes with the special therapies might cause you to be jealous. It's OK to feel this way—talk to your parents and they'll help you address those feelings. Depending on your family size and structure, your parents might be able to arrange special time with just you. The most important thing to remember is that it's OK to feel this way, but make sure you talk to someone about how you feel.

Lesson 7: It's OK to have interests separate from your sibling

As you grow up, it will be important to keep yourself separate from your sibling. You're your own person. I have many activities that I do without my brother. First, I'm a runner and my brother isn't. I run several days each week, and I have long runs on the weekend. I don't feel guilty when I head out for my runs because my runs are for me. When I was in school, I was a cheerleader. We had practice every day and during the summer we practiced twice each day. My brother really wanted to come to those activities! However, my mother wanted to make sure he didn't crowd my life, and she allowed cheerleading to be mine alone.

Develop hobbies and interests that are separate. These will be things that are yours that you don't have to share. You can always introduce your brother or sister to your preferred activities, but you don't have to.

Your career is also yours and doesn't have to be shared with anyone. Choose a career that interests *you* and makes *you* happy, not your parents. Billy Ray Cyrus helped his daughter Miley to develop a career doing what she loves. You should do the same, and it's OK if it has nothing to do with autism.

Lesson 8: It's OK to dislike autism

If you're old enough to read this book, you've been around long enough to have learned quite a bit about autism and all it brings to a family. You should be the first to know there's nothing about autism you have to like. None of us *likes* autism. If given the choice, we would eradicate autism from the planet. However, for the time being, autism is in the world, and it's in *our* world, impacting *our* family, and no one else will understand until it affects their family like it's touched ours.

Just so you know, researchers don't like autism. That's why we're all fighting so hard to find a cure. If a cure for autism were to be found, the researchers would be delighted to find another area to study.

Parents don't like autism either. Autism is expensive and stressful for parents, and it keeps them awake at night. Many parents have spent every penny they have to try to cure their child with autism.

Every sibling I've met in my lifetime doesn't like autism. I often wonder if I would like my brother as much if he didn't have autism. I do know that many things about our lives would be better if his autism were gone.

Lesson 9: Enjoy your sibling with autism

The most important lesson I've learned over the years is to enjoy Mac. He brings many, many challenges, but most of all he also brings unconditional love. He still enjoys my company even if I get mad at him, jealous of him, or tease him like a sibling.

We have so many activities we do together, just the two of us. For example, when we go swimming together, he holds my hands and jumps up and down three times before he goes under the water. When he comes up, he laughs hysterically. When we go to amusement parks, we ride the swings together several times. When we go to community parks, we like to race on the hiking trail. We'll count down, take off running, and laugh when we stop after tiring. Our favorite activity together is dancing. I made a playlist of all of his favorite songs. Whenever I play his songs, he gets very excited and he asks me to snap and clap with him.

Over the years, you'll develop special routines you can do, just the two of you. Learn to enjoy all of the unique things you'll have because of your sibling.

Part II

For Teenagers and Parents

14

Susannah Chandler, Age 22

When I was ten years old, I decided I wished my brother had never been born. I didn't hate or resent him—I knew it wasn't his fault that he erupted in anger at the table almost nightly. Or that his two-hour-long visits to the bathroom often meant we left the house over an hour late. I knew I couldn't blame him for not being the sibling I wanted him to be. But, as callous as I knew it sounded, even in my own head, I felt my life would be better if he weren't a part of it.

It's not that we had a bad relationship. I was generally understanding, even when his actions hurt me, because I knew that, as hard as it was for me to have a sibling with autism, it was even harder for him actually to have it. I didn't feel anger at him so much as complete detachment and an awareness of what I'd lost by not having a "normal" brother.

When I looked at my friends' brothers, annoying and gross as my friends declared them to be, I was enchanted by the bond they shared. I envied not only the inside jokes and protection but even the teasing, because it hinted at a proximity I knew I could never reach with my own sibling. When I looked at him—pained, distant, stuttering—in addition to feeling bad for him that he'd never get to lead a normal life, I felt deeply robbed that I would never have what it seemed like every other family did.

Almost a decade has passed, and my feelings about my brother have changed completely.

I wish I could say this is all due to massive personal growth on my part. But, more than anything, my brother's successes have changed our relationship. Over the past ten years, he's not only survived but thrived, and is now doing well in a mainstream school. He's gone far beyond what I thought was possible for him.

When he was little, the odds seemed so heavily stacked against him that I saw no future for him outside of an institution. My parents have admitted that, at the time, his anger management was so poor they expected him to end up in jail. In my mind, my brother was a ticking time bomb—it was dangerous to get too attached to him. I thought his presence in my life was transient. There wasn't any real connection. Like any other challenging thing—a mean teacher, a bully in school—it was just something I had to get through. Watching him succeed beyond anything I thought possible has helped me to view him as a full person—and an extraordinary one.

I know his world is still a scary place. Background noises the rest of us don't even notice discomfit him. Prolonged social exposure unnerves him. His world is filled with annoyances and threats, not to mention prejudice. It wrenches my heart to think of how hard it is for him to get through a day. But the fact that he does it—that somehow, miraculously, he navigates his way through the world better than many of those deemed "normal"—astounds and inspires me. He's the bravest person I know; I can honestly say my brother is my hero.

We will never have what "normal" siblings have. I still don't know that I'd call us close in the traditional sense. But there are a lot of different kinds of love. Other siblings share secrets and hang out and team up against their parents. And there are still days when I'd give anything to have that. But today, I genuinely enjoy my time with him and treasure his presence in my life. When I think of my brother, I'm blown away by his resilience and courage, and I aspire to face the world with even half as much strength as he does.

And who's to say our kind of love isn't even better?

15

Rebecca Sicile-Kira, Age 17

Jeremy and Rebecca

When I reflect upon having a sibling with autism, an assortment of thoughts, both positive and negative, comes to mind. There are many aspects that are difficult to deal with, but at the same time there are many positives too. I felt there was no better way to share these aspects than by making a list.

Pros	Cons
Through my brother's autism I've become exposed to a significant amount of information and have learned a lot about it, which I wouldn't have done if I hadn't had a sibling with autism.	It might not be the case with all those with autism, but for my brother the autism means he has no sense of personal space. This causes him to go through my things, unaware he's crossing a boundary. Because of this, I've had to keep all my objects either locked up or hidden away.
Instead of just focusing on autism, his disability has encouraged me to study other disabilities and take classes such as psychology to further my interest in other behavioral differences.	When I was younger, I was constantly embarrassed when others would point, stare, and make comments about my brother's odd habits. Now that I'm older I'm no longer embarrassed, but I definitely remember feeling humiliated at times when I was younger.
Dealing with the hardships that come from having a sibling with autism has allowed me to be much more patient and understanding when it comes to other people who are different.	One negative attribute has been the spontaneous behavior. When it's hot, there's a full moon, or some other reason that cannot be determined, my brother is unable to sleep. Instead of staying quietly in his room, he gets up and tends to wake up the rest of us. This can be quite annoying, especially when I have to wake up early the next morning.
Last, my brother's autism has allowed me to be truly grateful for the life I'm able to live. My brother will never have some of the same experiences I've taken for granted. This has made me appreciate my life, and what I'm able to accomplish, much more.	The final con of having a sibling with autism is the lack of a "typical" sibling relationship— at times this has been very disappointing for me.

It's definitely not easy to grow up with a sibling who has autism. Since my brother is older than me, it always felt wrong helping him out, when he should have been the one guiding me. Being the youngest, I always felt I should be the one given the most attention, but I quickly learned my brother was the one who needed and deserved it the most. I've struggled a lot through my childhood to understand and accept my brother's autism, and still to this day I get frustrated and annoyed.

Instead of just viewing a sibling's autism in a negative light, it's vital to consider the positive side of living with someone with a disability. Sure, there are some minor rewards such as being able to cut the line at Disneyland, but having a sibling with autism provides an environment that's highly uncommon. Let's face it, not many teens are able to say they've recently seen almost every single *Sesame Street* video because their 20-year-old brother still watches them.

Much knowledge can be gained from this experience, and it gives us an upper hand at many things later in life. Many people will go through their entire life without experiencing what we have. It's taken me most of my childhood to realize the advantage I have over others. I've developed an assortment of personality traits and have learned to be more patient and mature in certain situations. Now that I've started to apply to colleges and write my personal essays, I realize that my experience with my brother's autism has provided me with a unique life experience and has given me a mature outlook on life.

Rebecca and her brother Jeremy were featured on the MTV show *True Life: I Have Autism.*

16

Jenna Cohen, Age 24

When I was five years old, I didn't know what autism was. I don't think anyone in my family really knew. All I knew was I was getting a baby sister and I was excited! I remember my dad picking me and my little sister Lisa up to go to the hospital to see our new sister, Michelle. Michelle was diagnosed with autism a few years later, and my life is different because of it.

When I was ten years old, boy, did I know all about autism. I was making lots of new friends, but it was hard for me to invite them over. What would I tell them about Michelle? I was shy, and autism still wasn't well known then, and I didn't know how to explain it to any of my friends. How does one kid tell another kid about autism? I don't think it stopped me from seeing my friends and having them over, but it sure did make me uncomfortable at times.

When I was 15, I knew even more about autism. I had a rough time during one year in high school, and I thought Michelle was part of the reason. I was jealous that my parents spent more time and effort on her, jealous that they coached her teams and led her Girl Scout troop. It's not easy being the oldest. I was also angry and sad that I didn't have much of a relationship with Michelle—the only times we played together were when we were running and sliding around on the kitchen floor.

When I was 20, I lived away from home at college. I had the time of my life. I majored in psychology and also ended up choosing a minor in disability studies, in large part because of Michelle. But I also had to start thinking about what kind of a job I wanted after college. At the time I thought I wanted to go to graduate school, and I thought long and hard about what it was in particular I wanted to study. In the end I decided on autism—I was interested in learning about what makes kids with autism develop so differently from other kids. What is it that's different in their brains?

Now I'll be turning 25, and I'm still interested in studying autism but mainly on my own time. I have a job doing something else and I think there are plenty of other people out there who want to study and learn about autism, so it's OK if I don't. I live about three and a half hours away from my parents and Michelle, and that makes it harder. It's difficult for me because it's still hard to have a relationship with her. It still makes me angry and sad sometimes. It's one sided—I always have to go to her, but she won't really come to me. It also hurts that my parents can't just hop in the car and come visit like a lot of my friends' parents can—instead they have to plan the trip carefully to make sure Michelle will be OK. (I also know my parents didn't choose this and they probably have many of the same feelings I do.)

My parents really are the most kind and patient people I know, and they're perfect for Michelle. We're lucky to have them as parents. I'm also lucky I have Lisa, who probably understands better than anyone else. It's hard for me to talk about it with my family, but when I do, it helps. Recently I was having a conversation with a friend who was complaining about his younger sister and how she didn't go to college and wasn't really doing anything with her life, and how he didn't like that. It brought me to tears because all I could think was that I would give anything for that to be Michelle. Sitting here writing this, it might sound as if I've had more pain than pleasure, but I don't feel that's the case. I think I struggle so much because I love her so much. That's just the way it is, the way it always will be.

17

Lisa Cohen, Age 21

Michelle

When we were young,
innocence overwhelmed me.
I didn't understand
that you didn't understand.

We grew up playing together,
running around the house,
dancing to music and taking walks outside.
Bonding through our childhood games,
I began to learn how you learn.

You make weird noises—in public,
people stare.
I cherish the times we spend together,
but it's not the same as my friends and their siblings.
You are different:
the red rose growing in a patch of yellow tulips.

Shuttling you to gymnastics practice and back,
listening to the same song five times on the way,
teaching you to give high-fives,
to play computer games and bake brownies,
learning to be patient was inevitable.

You are a puzzle and I am slowly putting together the
pieces.
Little Sister, I'll show you the world if you let me.

Protecting you from the outside world—
they do not understand.
As an adult I feel responsibility
for the child that is living in your adult body.

Little Sister,
I did not realize until I felt responsibility
that I have felt acceptance for you
since my days of innocence.

18

Hannah Burke, Age 15

Dad, Nathanael, Mom, Hannah, and Michael

I don't think I could name one specific thing that's hardest about having siblings with autism. But near the top of the list is being pushed away by family, friends, and even people we don't really know, all because we're not "easy." For example, we can't go to birthday parties because if one of my brothers got a scoop of ice cream or a piece of cake, he could become brain-damaged. People just don't believe that—they think it's ridiculous and absurd, and aren't willing to alter their menu to accommodate my brothers' allergies.

Another major thing is all the work. I don't know about you, but I wouldn't call teaching four- and six-year-olds how to talk and play, and do your average, normal things everyone takes for granted, "a lazy summer afternoon." It always surprises me when I'm around "normal" four-to-six-year-olds how much they talk and play. Even three-year-olds seem to carry on conversations better than my six-year-old brother does! It's horrible for me to watch "normal" kids because I desperately want my little brothers to be able to do the things those other kids can do. I had a little boy start a conversation with me not too long ago. He was probably about three. He was with his baby sister outside the restrooms in a store and he told me about how his hair had grown "lots of days," and his sister's hair had grown "lots of days," and his mommy's hair had grown "lots of days," and his daddy's hair had grown "lots of days." When he told me he was waiting for his mommy, I told him I was waiting for my mommy too. He looked at me in awe, and said, "You have a mommy?" My brothers don't do things like that, ever, and it hurts. But we want them to. I know this is why we do what we do. That's why we work so hard to heal my brothers. This is why we take them to therapies several hours away and try constantly to interact with them. So that someday, when the cashier at the store says something friendly to them, they can respond.

Honestly, though, four of the most dreaded words in the English language have got to be "Interact with your brothers." It's not that I don't love them and want them to be better, and even want to play with them: it can just feel so overwhelming and pointless and frustrating. I so often wish I had the energy just to take on the world and never become so exhausted that all I honestly care about is sleep.

Of course, I could probably have more energy if I wasn't allergic to coffee beans and could drink caffeinated mochas all day. Ooh, that sounds delicious. Not only am I allergic to coffee, I'm also allergic to dairy and gluten and peanut butter and strawberries and eggs and, well, the list goes on, as it does for my brothers. Let's just say broccoli doesn't qualify as comfort food. Siblings often have similar gut problems to their brother or sister on the autism spectrum. I'm no exception. So the whole mocha thing (with whipped cream and chocolate) is a fantasy that's up there with having an extended family again.

I'm lucky, in a sense, because my parents haven't gotten divorced like so many in our situation, but not *so* lucky, because I lost my extended family. I used to have an extended family. Holidays were a big thing. On my mom's side of the family, there were my two aunts, two uncles, their kids, my single aunt, a family whom we kind of adopted, and sometimes close friends. I remember everyone always coming together at Easter. We would make and frost sugar cookies. I remember gift exchanges at Christmas, and lots of birthday parties. The single aunt moved away. On my dad's side, the only one involved is his mom. She tries to understand and be supportive of our fight against autism. She even comes over with organic fruit instead of cookies. I wish the rest of my family made as much effort. But she's just one person in our entire family. And as our lives became less normal and we focused more on recovering my brothers, everyone else decided they didn't want to be bothered with us any more. I guess having cornbread stuffing for Thanksgiving dinner is more important to them than being a family to us.

So the family I used to feel so connected to has dumped us. The church family, on the other hand, didn't dump us. They were never there. Sure, if my parents ask the elders or pastors to pray for us or give them advice, they will, but whoopee-day. I often hear people say, "We're praying for you!" And I always think, "Shut up. You don't even *know*, and I highly doubt you *are* praying for us." Or someone will say to one of my parents, "I could never do what you do." But I think they could if they had to.

You can choose to do one of three things when faced with an autism spectrum disorder. You can stick your kid in an institution, where he'll be strapped to a bed 24/7, and worse; you can passively accept your child's autism and say, "Oh that's just who he is," and live with it, not doing anything until he dies. Or you can try to fix your broken baby. That's what we're doing: fixing our two broken babies. Kids develop autism because their bodies become so overloaded with toxins they can no longer function correctly. They don't have enough of a natural antioxidant called glutathione, which we all need to get toxins out of our bodies. They aren't mentally disabled.

There was a time when I searched for a friend who understood autism—someone else who was my age who had a sibling with autism. I asked my mom to ask around on her autism list-serve. I went to a support group once called "Sib Shop." But the list-serve proved fruitless and the Sib Shop was the same day every month as my mom's TACA (Talk About Curing Autism) meeting, so it didn't work out. The kids at Sib Shop seemed fairly clueless about what affects their siblings. They seemed to live their own lives apart from autism, unlike me—I'm immersed in it.

It seems as if people, friends, therapists, or acquaintances expect me, as a 15-year-old, to be somehow separate from my brothers. They assume I have my own life. But I don't, and I'm kind of glad. Because, otherwise, I wouldn't know all these cool things like how non-organic cow's milk has pus in it because of what they're fed, and if your cheeks are really red, you're probably eating something you're allergic to. Or that guy who seriously looks pregnant only looks like that because he has severe yeast overgrowth.

Right now I'm trying to read about the Specific Carbohydrate Diet (SCD), which is kind of boring and technical, but great too! I want to learn all about treatments that help cure autism so I can talk about it and not sound like a dummy. I've listened to Jenny McCarthy's *Louder than Words* on CD and read parts of her newest book, *Healing and Preventing Autism* with Dr. Jerry Kartzinel. Reading that book through is next on my list. The chapters that I read were out loud to my mom during car rides to therapies. I "lucked out" and got to read a whole chapter on poop (because that's where she happened to be in that book at the time). It was gross. Mom let me skip over the suppository part (bless her heart and my mind).

Something that frustrates me is that the media conversation is all about the parents. Most of the time the mom. You hear about "Mother Warriors." Moms defeating autism! Support groups for moms! Credit it all to the moms! The siblings just get taken for granted. I mean, why don't you see 15-year-olds on *Larry King Live* or *Oprah* sharing *their* stories? After all, it's us siblings who get the brunt of Mom's emotional devastation from having something go wrong with her other child and feeling as if it's her fault. Or the anger she has toward her hard life. Or the effects of sleepless nights. Or a million other things!

Sometimes I feel terribly sorry for myself. Sometimes I can't think of one good thing in my life. Like on the days when my mom is yelling at me, and we have places to go, and I feel tired and depressed, and Michael is screaming his head off, and Nathanael is acting like a space cadet. Those are the really horrible days. When I'm around other teens who have normal, annoying siblings who go to regular school and act like dumb, typical teens, I realize how much I live in my own world, how much I've been isolated. I feel so different from all those other kids who have a comparatively normal life. Once, my best friend Hailee commented to me, "Wow, Hannah, you need to get out more." It was in a totally different context—I hadn't gotten a joke she'd pulled—but it stung because that's how I felt. I'd love to "get out more." But I live in a small town, my parents are very protective, and I live with autism, which is a 24/7 job. "Getting out more" in any context other than going to the store or to different places for different therapies is impossible.

It feels as if I really get a break when I go to my best friend's house. In that, I'm really lucky. Going over there is a break for me, even if Hailee isn't around, because I enjoy every member of her family and I'm not at *my* house with *my* family. I would even be perfectly satisfied spending the day with her parents, but I don't think they get that. Hailee seems to have only just noticed I even *have* brothers. I adore her parents, but as adults they have their own issues to deal with—they don't need mine, nor could they truly understand them. Her little brother is only 11, and I expect nothing out of him except that he'll try to insult me in some way, shape, or form, which I'm perfectly fine with. It just means I torture him by giving him hugs. Her older brother, who is 15, will listen to what I say without comment, which doesn't exactly help soothe the nobody-understands-me sensation. So, although I get great support from that family because I know they love me, they'll never be able to empathize.

I also have a close friend who lives in a different state. I can tell her anything and she'll try to sympathize, but, like everyone else, she doesn't get it. You have to experience autism to understand it. However, she always asks me how I'm doing, how my brothers are doing, how my family is doing. I love that because I know she really cares.

That's not to say I love it when *everyone* asks. For instance—Therapist: "How has your week been?" Me: "Fine." Like what, I'm going to tell you my world is in pieces and I'm sick of people like you who smile way too much? You don't care about me. Most people don't really care when they ask you how you're doing. At least, not the people I'm around. Have you ever noticed that although some therapists are great, some of them act fake? Like, stop smiling at me. Why are you smiling at me? You don't even know me.

So how do I cope with autism? Well, most of the time I don't. These days anger and sorrow make up a good 70 percent of my emotions. I feel angry a lot. Angry that I'm not able to pursue dreams, and angry that I miss out on so many things I want to be a part of. I also often feel depressed or sad. There was a point when I was constantly feeling depressed and I figured out that taking vitamin D and iron really helps. Sometimes I'll cry. Depending on her mood, either my mom will tell me to quit being self-pitying or she'll just let me do my thing. Once in a while she'll even ask me if I need to cry. If I look sad, my dad always asks me what's wrong. A lot of the time I feel he's more supportive than my mom.

It's also good for me to remember life isn't about me, it's about everyone. Although realizing that's great, remembering it is another story. I just have to be OK with the fact that my world revolves around my brothers. Another thing is that I'll be 18 in three years—though that thought is mostly scary, and I certainly wouldn't forsake my family like so many have done.

So I really think I lucked out in a lot of ways. I have great parents when they aren't making me mad; I have a "family of friends;" I have a friend who lives several states away who I can talk to (even if she doesn't get it); I have two adorable, wonderful brothers; and I have God. He's a big one. Because the Maker of the stars can hear the sound of my breaking heart. Sometimes that single thought is all it takes to comfort me.

And you know what? I can cope with losing my extended family. I'm OK with feeling like the odd teenager out. I know a lot for being only 15. Not necessarily academically speaking, but in the things that count. I'm growing up a little every day and I can feel it. I can see it. I think it's partly because autism is giving me a different vantage point. I'm not as self-absorbed as I might otherwise be. I'm getting thicker skin from having to deal with all the frustration and hurt that comes from being constantly tried and tested. I'm getting a broader view of life from being around so many different personalities in the form of doctors and therapists of all different sorts. And sitting in a car for hours on end provides a person with some major soul-searching time. Or I can just exercise my imagination. I've also decided that if I ever become rich, I'm adopting an autistic kid and recovering him or her.

Speaking of raising kids, I love it when people comment on how well behaved and obedient my brothers are. (Of course, people have also commented on how quiet I am and my mom's response is "You don't live with her.") But, really, my brothers are great. They *are* well behaved and obedient. Parents sometimes use autism as an excuse for not correcting their child—just letting them do whatever they want to keep the peace. That's not how my brothers have been raised, so they aren't obnoxious kids. (Well, Michael has been screaming a whole lot lately and that's really, really obnoxious, but, other than that, they're nice to be around. OK, well, Nathanael has a tendency to grab hold of cashiers' nametags and pull them down, but I promise it's not because he actually wants to see their cleavage. That's just a side effect. He likes the letters that are on the nametag.)

Michael, the four-year-old, can read. Nathanael can read too, but he's not really crazy about it. Michael, in addition to reading and writing, draws. Nathanael likes to build trains, tracks, and bridges with blocks. He only recently started doing that. Michael loves meat; Nathanael would be OK with being a vegetarian. Nathanael has this very impish, teasing personality. Michael is emotional. Nathanael has freckles sprinkled over his face; Michael has no freckles. Michael is very strong. In fact, he could hold himself rigid when he was born. I think that has something to do with too much testosterone. Nathanael is small—no bigger than Michael. Before he developed autism at two and a half years old, Michael and I had a cool bond. I would sit and hold him for the longest time or we would fall asleep on the couch together. So while Mom was totally focused on Nathanael, I paid more attention to Michael. After Michael had his complete turnaround that took him from happy, talkative baby to hiding in the closet, we stayed bonded for a little while. Thanks to autism, we no longer have that same bond. I've always loved and doted on Nathanael, but he's Mamma's boy. I'd rather play with Nathanael than Michael because Nathanael is older and acts like it, even if he doesn't carry on conversation. So, both my brothers, though they're not "normal," have very distinct personalities, and I love them totally and completely. I will forever, whether they get better or get worse. Even if my parents grow old and die and my brothers still have autism, I'll love them and take care of them. Meanwhile, I'll just continue more or less as I have. Sometimes I'll break down, sometimes I'll handle it well, and for me, my version of "happily ever after" will be for my brothers to become normal. But I would settle for being able to have a conversation with them.

Christine Hurd, Age 18

Christine

You grow up more quickly when you have an autistic sibling.

"Babysitting" takes on a different meaning. Instead of the vague responsibility of calling 911 for Poison Control or the Fire Department if a horrible accident were to happen, you have *rules*. Many, many rules. And there are serious consequences if these rules aren't followed perfectly.

For example, a diet infraction can lead to a three-hour meltdown. Is your sister hungry? How about some milk and cookies? Except you can't give them to her. Because she can't have milk. Or wheat or corn or soy or most vegetables and fruit. She can eat rice, but she gets bored with that. You would too if your plate were a dreary grayish white, full of rice cakes and potato.

As for a routine, good luck. Pushing your sibling to do basic things such as use the bathroom or swallow medication can lead to gigantic tantrums. Your friends gripe about their brothers and sisters giving them a tough time or not being fair or nice. *Your* sibling will bite your hand so hard the bones might break. However, instead of normal sibling fights, you can't bite, hit, or scratch back. But you can't walk away either. If you leave, she'll blacken her eyes, bloody her hands, bruise her body past purple and black and blue.

So when things are tough, you hold her and say it'll be OK. Chant that it will be OK. Everything will be *O-K*. Would she like a song? Snack? Game? No. She just doesn't want to hurt inside. You don't want it either.

You're angry this happened to your sibling, your family, yourself. You're afraid of what the future will be like—a future without your parents. You're just afraid in general.

Don't be. It doesn't last.

For me, high school ended the fear. Academics provided a path that could help my sister. By studying math, chemistry, and biology, I could try to understand autism. I could prepare myself for a career that would help her; I could be a doctor or a scientist or a lawyer or a teacher. The future became full.

And when fear didn't haunt my thoughts, I saw my sister differently. I'd seen her as an impossible challenge, never improving or changing or living. Now, I see her for the beautiful person she is and will be.

She's musical and full with laughter. She sprawls out on the sand, the grinning girl in the magazine. She loves to swim. She loves the feeling of the grass. She smiles and giggles when you lift her up into her swing. She closes her eyes in the sun and lifts her hands in the air as if to grab the rays. She loves everything good: nature and wind, movement and music, food and family.

It was a circle. I'd feel hope for the future and see my sister progress, and then feel inspired to do more and then see the results. I became proud to be her friend and protector.

I'd like to think this emotional change was part of a big plan, the plan where "everything is going to be OK," and where we both don't have to hurt any more.

But really, it's because you grow up more quickly when you have a sibling you love.

CPSIA information can be obtained at www.ICGtesting.com
Printed in the USA
BVOW06s1248080615

403486BV00008B/54/P